Learn the Art of Winning Sales Letters

Elena Adani

Kevin Turner

DEDICATION

Dear reader, thank you so much for having purchased this book. Mr. Kevin Turner and Mrs. Elena Adani will guide you to discover the secret of writing a persuasive and winning Sales Letter from scratch.

We recommend you to read this book carefully, feel free to get in touch with Elena or Kevin by email, to this address elena@lifenowacademy.com anytime you want. Kevin and Elena will be glad to give you their support during your sales adventures and give you advice for you to become a winner in your sales' niche.

Enjoy reading.

Elena Adani
Kevin Turner

CONTENTS

1 THE WINNING SALES LETTER

In this chapter, we will see an example of a sales letter about a video course teaching the same topics this book explains. You will see that this sales letter consists of different steps that we will analyze throughout this book.

Let's go and look at this example of the sales letter of the course "Learn the Art of Winning Sales Letters."

STEP ONE – THE HEADLINE

Do you want the sales of your product to explode, and do you want to be recognized as one of the leading experts in your industry?

**Learn the art of winning sales letters
And increase your Sales dramatically**

STEP TWO – PRESENTATION OF THE PROBLEM

If you like to stand out in the market and have the success you deserve in sales, having a product or service that solves the problems of your customers is not enough alone. You also need to create a trust relationship with them and make them fall in love with your offer. That is why it's essential to communicate effectively with your customers and learn how to write winning sales letters.

I know how you feel when, after having worked hard, the results you expect are late to arrive. Sometimes your competitors conquer the market, although they have a product that is less valid than yours is. This situation creates frustrations, worry, discomfort, and tiredness.

It is like being trapped inside a hamster wheel; you keep on running without getting anywhere. The uncertainty and doubt prevent you from thinking clearly and finding the right way to increase the sales of your product.

All of this creates stress; maybe you cannot sleep at night. Your future and that of your family depends on the sales you will achieve. You have what it takes to succeed, but you feel something is missing, and despite your commitment, the goal still seems far away. If you are experiencing a similar situation, it is time to seriously take into consideration the importance of the marketing and communication of your business, and avoid wasting time and money continuing to delegate this responsibility to others. Why keep on repeating the same mistakes that the majority of entrepreneurs make, such as: **do not personally undertake the marketing and sale of their products?**

To entirely delegate the advertising of your product to a marketing agency or consultant is a mistake that I recommend you avoid.

You can have the most effective product in the world to sell; however, to convince your customers to buy it, you have to sell yourself first and build a trust relationship with them. Who is better placed to do this than you?

If you take full responsibility for the communication and marketing of your company, you can change your strategy each time to pursue your goal, without spending money to delegate this responsibility to others entirely. It doesn't mean that you have to end the collaborations with the marketing agencies or consultants you are working with. Even the most skilled and famous marketing experts always ask for advice from a peer group.

STEP THREE – WHO ARE YOU AND WHY SHOULD THE CUSTOMER TRUST IN YOU

A few years ago, I also did not believe the importance of learning to communicate and introduce my services winningly. Then one day, I finally understood that, if I hadn't committed to mastering the art of persuasion and marketing, I could never leave my job to start a new business. I was willing to get in the game at any cost, despite having no guarantee of success.

When I worked as an employee in the sales office of a services company, I felt like a beast locked in a cage, continually searching for a way out. Then, I decided that I had enough.

My suffering forced me to choose between living a life full of dissatisfaction and sadness or striving for my happiness and fulfillment even at the professional level.

Thanks to the help of a life coach, I found the courage to end the relationship with my partner, and I also quit my job. Then, I became a coach too, I wrote two books, and I started to fall in love with digital marketing, and I finally created the job that I had always wanted.

Marketing and winning writing has allowed me to understand the human mind better and to introduce my ideas and products in a unique, innovative way, and overcome the fear of being judged. I have been doing coaching, marketing, and self-esteem consulting for a few years, and the results that I'm having have passed my optimistic expectations.

"Who would have ever thought that Elena Adani, who when she was a teenager had bad self-esteem and was often teased by others because she was too introverted, would have been able to take back the power of her own life and make such a radical change?".

STEP FOUR – INTRODUCE YOUR SOLUTION

You can also achieve success by learning to introduce your product and yourself attractively and improve your relationship with your customers. When they read your sales letters, they will look forward to working with you. To write sales letters, you do not need to become a writer of best sellers or studying marketing for years. Just commit regularly and follow the steps of the course **"Learn the Art of Winning Sales Letters."**

To be successful in your business, your customers need to feel your presence, even if they do not know you. For this reason, the course "Learn the Art of Winning Sales Letters" is the only one that talks about self-esteem and gives you practical exercises to create the best conditions for you to deal with your customers. There is no point denying that what you feel has a high impact on all your relationships, both personal and professional.

Furthermore, taking the time to write your sales letters will help to avoid committing another mistake that, unfortunately, many entrepreneurs make: **focusing too much on their products' characteristics, without knowing how to convince their customers to buy them.**

We often forget that men and women make decisions only when emotions drive them. The most skilled marketing experts in the world know this, and that's the reason why they know the human psyche very well and how to involve the audience emotionally.

So, how to learn all of this?

STEP FIVE – YOUR PRODUCT

The course **"Learn the Art of Winning Sales Letters"** is the only marketing course that explains all of the secrets to writing a sales letter from scratch. I will guide you step-by-step in every phase of writing and will suggest you the more effective sales and communication strategies to you. In this course, I will give you all of the most effective tools to:

- ✓ Understand how important Self-esteem is during the sales process and how to improve it.
- ✓ Provide you with a track to create the identikit of your ideal customer and describe your product in an effective manner.
- ✓ Create a captivating Headline to intrigue your audience to keep on reading your sales letter and find out more.
- ✓ Agitate the problem so the customers will be aware of the consequences that they will have to face if they do not take any action to solve it.
- ✓ How to tell your story to your customers so they will trust you and the solution you offer. Before evaluating a product, people have to rely on the person or the company that sells it. Therefore, before selling your product, you have to become skilled in selling yourself.
- ✓ Introduce the advantages of your product, and how to differentiate yourself in the market, so that your customers will prefer your offer instead of others.
- ✓ Learn to communicate appealingly.
- ✓ Transform any imperfection or limitation of your product into strength.
- ✓ Provide positive reviews from your satisfied customers to build confidence.

✓ Provide a guarantee and bonuses to encourage customers to make the purchase immediately.
✓ Make a general summary of the most critical parts of your proposal.
✓ How to push the customers to accept your offer through a captivating "Call to action."

If you want to stand out from the competition, become more skilled in marketing, improve the relationship with your customers using a captivating communication, learn how to respond appropriately to any objection they could make. If you like to possess a useful marketing tool to increase the sales of your product or service, then the course "Learn the Art of Winning Sales Letters" is for you.

However, if for any reason you think that is useless to take these actions, I suggest you to stop reading this introduction now and let go of the course "Learn the Art of Winning Sales Letters" because it is not for people who:

✓ Are not willing to undertake the marketing of their company.
✓ Do not want to learn the rules of persuasion.
✓ Are convinced that just having the right product is enough to sell it.
✓ Ignore the importance of sales letters and winning communication in their marketing strategy.
✓ Completely delegate their marketing strategies to marketing agencies or consultants without giving their support.

- ✓ Are convinced that their personal story and experiences are not interesting for their audience.
- ✓ Feel worthless to create a trust relationship with their potential customers.

Wouldn't you feel happier and satisfied knowing that dedicating a few hours to write your message, you help increase the sales of your products and be appreciated even by people you have never met?

Wouldn't it be great to feel this incredible sense of well-being every day?

STEP SIX – PRICE AND BONUSES

Your customers will find you due to the effectiveness of your marketing and will love you, not only because you are a handsome man or a beautiful woman but for the positive emotions that you'll be able to arouse in them.

Then what are you waiting for, it is time to take the first step to your success.

The course "Learn the Art of Winning Sales Letters" is now available at the special price of

$ 97,00

But that's not all; the price includes:

BONUS 1

The book "Be the Hero of Your Life" – An

Instruction Manual for Self-esteem. $ 13,00

In this book, you will find practical exercises to increase your self-esteem and discover the subconscious mind traps. It will be beneficial to tackle any objection your customers may have.

BONUS 2

One hour online free consultation with me, to help you to define your marketing strategy and write your sales letter   **$ 150,00**

Bonuses total Price	**$ 163,00**
TOTAL PRICE	**$ 260,00**

Of course, you will not have to pay   **$ 260,00**

The course "Learn the Art of Winning Sales Letters" plus the book "Be the Hero of Your Life," plus the online free consulting will be yours
          at the incredible price of $ 97,00

Take advantage of this offer because it will only be valid until July 30th, 2019. After that date, the price will go up, and I still have not decided if and when I will do another promotion on this course.

STEP SEVEN – REVIEWS

As you can see, I have set this introduction as if it were a sales letter, so at this point, I should write reviews from satisfied customers about this course. I want to be extremely sincere with you and tell you that I cannot write any review now, because this course sale starts in September 2019. I could have invented some reviews and written them down here, but I prefer you to be the one giving me a review so I can share it here with your permission.

STEP EIGHT – GUARANTEE

If, at the end of this course, you have not learned how to create at least one draft of your sales letter, do not worry, I will refund you 100% of the price you have paid for it. However, I'm sure that you will not ask for any guarantee. If you strictly follow every step of this course, it is impossible not to learn how to write a captivating sales letter.

STEP NINE – SUMMARY

Let's sum this up.
If you want:
- ✓ avoid getting discouraged if you are not reaching the sales goals that you expected.
- ✓ Stop waste time and money entrusting others to your marketing strategy.
- ✓ Possess a useful marketing tool to increase your sales.
- ✓ Learn the art of persuasion and how to write a winning sales letter from scratch.

✓ Establish trust and lasting relationships with your customers.

✓ Make the customers fall in love with your offer so that they will prefer your product or service instead of others.

✓ Intrigue your customers to keep on reading your sales letter and push them to make the purchase immediately.

Get the course "Learn the Art of Winning Sales Letters" plus

Bonus no.1 the book "Be the Hero of Your Life" plus

Bonus no.2 the online free consulting at the incredible price of $ 97,00

This offer is valid until July 30, 2019

P.S.

Learning to write winning sales letters will not automatically guarantee you an increase in sales because this will also depend on your marketing strategies. However, you can invest all of the time and money you like in learning your preferred marketing strategies, but if you do not learn to communicate with your customers in a certain way, and correctly write your sales letters, you won't be able to convince your readers to trust you and buy your product.

So, are you willing to accept this challenge?

STEP TEN – CALL TO ACTION

Don't miss this incredible offer, take advantage of the **special price of $ 97,00** to get the course **"Learn the Art of Winning Sales Letters"** including the two bonuses (the book "Be the Hero of Your Life" plus the online free consulting).

Before evaluating a product or a service, people have to rely on the person or on the company that sells it. For this reason, the course "Learn the Art of Winning Sales Letters" will teach you **how to be loved by your audience, and how to introduce your product appealingly.**

Take the chance of becoming a skilled seller, and learn the art of persuasion to establish with your audience a trust relationship and increase the sales of your products.

Warning: this is the last chance you have to take advantage of the course "Learn the Art of Winning Sales Letters," only investing $ 97,00.

This offer will be valid only until **July 30th, 2019**, after that date, the price will go up, and I still have not decided if and when there will be other promotions.

STEP ELEVEN – CONCLUSION

Thank you for having read up to this point. I hope that you can achieve your goals using all the sales tools you feel comfortable with. Any decision you will take on this course, please remember that I will always be at your disposal.

You can get in touch with me whenever you want on the site https://lifenowacademy.com or by email: elena@lifenowacademy.com
I wish you great success and wealth.

2 LET'S START WITH YOU

Before starting the practical part of this course, I would like to talk to you about the importance of self-esteem in the sales process. When you sell, write, recite, create, cook, or do any other action, your energy always manifests outside of you, and mostly depends on the thoughts and emotions that you feel. People close to you perceive this energy, especially at an unconscious level. Your thoughts and your feelings will always show outside of you, even if not verbally communicated, and determine the results you get. For this reason, when you promote your product on the market, it is crucial that you believe in what you do, that you keep positive thoughts, and have good self-esteem. Perhaps you may not believe what I've just said, especially if it is the first time you've heard anybody discuss these topics.

Usually, you have doubts; however, in recent years these theories have been widely demonstrated, even by quantum physics, in particular, Albert Einstein. According to Einstein, the thought is energy and can influence every aspect of your existence, more than you expect.

If you do not believe that thoughts and emotions are crucial for your success, try this experiment when you have the chance. Try to cook food when you're sick or angry, depressed, or sad, and then note the difference in the same dish that you prepare when you're in good shape and feeling happy. Even if you're not a skilled cook, I bet that in the first case, the taste of the food will be less pleasant than the one that you cooked with love and psychophysical performance. If you know a chef or you have the opportunity to speak to one, he/she will confirm what I have just said. This principle applies to any activities, therefore feel free to perform the same experiment in other contexts and note the difference between the results.

I'm talking about thoughts, emotions, and energy because very few marketing courses cover these topics, most do not bother to explain how important the psychophysical conditions of the sellers are. Indeed it is necessary to study the mind of the customer and learn the techniques of persuasion to be successful in the sale. However, it is equally important to put yourself in the shoes of the seller to understand what the seller feels and thinks. Motivation and enthusiasm are not enough alone to conclude good business. It is necessary to have good self-esteem, that will help you when you face challenging situations when the customer raises objections, and the competition will do everything to attack you. In these cases, your self-esteem will be your only anchor of salvation, to which you can hold on to overcome obstacles and avoid putting yourself down because of the judgment of others.

Always keep confidence in yourself and in what you do to preserve a good relationship with your customers. Your self-esteem must never falter.

Before starting to write any text or plan a marketing strategy, I suggest you follow the directions in the next exercise; this is the same exercise that you will find in chapter seven of my book "Be the Hero of Your life – An Instruction Manual for Self-esteem" available on Amazon.

EXERCISE 1

Choose a room or any place where you feel comfortable and are sure you won't be disturbed. This will be your self-esteem room. Take at least ten minutes a day to go to your self-esteem room. Get comfortable, lie down on the floor if you want, take deep breaths, and remember to correctly use your diaphragm (when you inhale your stomach should rise, while it should fall when you exhale).

If you feel it is necessary, listen to relaxation music. Take deep breaths until you eliminate any thought that distracts you. If you have difficulty freeing your mind, imagine your thoughts as white clouds that disappear into nothing, and then continue to breathe deeply while you get in touch with your deeper self. When you are relaxed and feel ready, imagine you are going down a set of stairs that lead you to a brightly lit room, there are many chests of drawers and shelves full of binders holding all of the information about you since you were born.

Concentrate on this image, designing it according to your likes and dislikes, every detail, from the color to the size. When you have your vision of the room perfectly designed, prepare for an unexpected meeting: a person dressed in white approaches you, smiling. You are surprised when you realize that person is you: it is your subconscious welcoming you to your headquarters. It wants to give you a hand in eliminating the thoughts, beliefs, and behaviors that have stopped you from having good self-esteem. Greet your subconscious and ask it to read the documents that describe episodes in your life in which you demonstrated your value. It could be your achievements, works, a game you won, a good relationship, or your school thesis, which was appreciated by all. Instead of showing you these documents, your subconscious does better.

It welcomes you to take a seat and watch a film showing you these scenes from your life. You can ask your subconscious to see the movie more than once, to strengthen your self-esteem.

After seeing your heroic feats, you ask your subconscious to keep these films available and to find similar ones. When you feel like your self-esteem, and the image you have of yourself has improved, say goodbye to your subconscious and leave the room. Watch yourself as you go back upstairs and return to the place you are in now. Slowly come back into contact with your body, making small movements with your hands and feet.

When you feel comfortable, open your eyes and take a deep

breath. After this exercise, it is preferable to remain in a relaxed position for a few minutes and not rush to work or do other stressful activities. Repeat this exercise as often as you like, without embellishing your noble endeavors.

As you can see, the visualization is so effective and powerful, the more you use it, the more you will appreciate its effectiveness. When you create a new product or a service, other than reaching good self-esteem, find clarity inside of yourself to understand the real motivations that allowed you to develop and sell it. Answer the questions in the following exercise; they will help you to plan an effective marketing strategy and write a winning sale letter.

Now that you have understood the importance of Self-esteem in the process of the sale, let's go to more in-depth into your mind, to understand the real motivations behind the creation of the product that you sell.

EXERCISE 2

1. What are the reasons that drove you to create and sell your product?
2. How did you feel while creating it?
3. Which specific problem do you want to resolve with your product?
4. Which example would you show to prove that your product is excellent?

Never lose faith in yourself and the potential of your product.

If you decide to improve it, then ask your customers to give you feedback, this helps to understand the needs of your audience better, differentiate yourself from your competitors, and create better products to satisfy your customer's requirements. Answering the questions of exercise No.2 will give you more incentives to start your deal with positive energy and a clear mind.

3 THE IDENTIKIT OF YOUR CUSTOMER

Emotions play a fundamental role in sales. Rarely a purchase happens in a completely automatic way. When we see an advertisement, we touch a product, or we read a sales letter; we always feel certain emotions, which lead us to make some choices. To make the first steps in the world of sales, you have to become familiar with the needs and thoughts of your potential customers.

During the various steps of this book, we will begin to understand the basic techniques to induce your customers to prefer your product over others. For this reason, I would like you to concentrate now on the **"uniqueness"** concept, and let go adjectives like **"better"** or **"worse"** because they are useless to you. Your success will depend mainly on your uniqueness and your ability to sell a "unique" and different product than others.

Now for convenience, I will use the word "Product" to identify any offerings, including services or consultations.

If today you are convinced that your product is useful for everybody, I highly recommend you modify it to make it different from the one of your competitors. Before writing your sales letter, it's vitally important that you carefully identify your niche in which you would like to work.

If you are not an expert in Google, for this step, it is useful to work with a consultant who will help you to find out the most searched keywords for similar products to yours, according to the geographical area you prefer. After having chosen the type of customers and the industry where you want to operate, it's time to create an Identikit of your customers, to fully understand what their needs are and how you can help to satisfy them. From now on, you have to become skilled in thinking like your customer. Imagine being him or her, and now you want to solve a specific problem, for example; find a nutritionist who can make you a customized diet to lose weight.

EXERCISE 3

Close your eyes for a few seconds and imagine yourself inside the mind of your customer. Answer the following questions:

1. What are the emotions your customers feel when they think of the problem that they want to solve?
2. What are their fears?
3. Why are they suffering now?
4. What are their biggest concerns?
5. Do they complain more often about anything?

6. Do some prejudices influence them?
7. What are their most profound desires that they want to satisfy?
8. Did they already buy a product or service similar to yours?
9. How much money do they have to buy your product?
10. What are the benefits that they will receive if they buy it?
11. What concerns or objections might they have about your product?
12. What are your competitors offering to them?

Don't be in a hurry to answer these questions. In this step, you will have to be very honest and ask yourself if your product is effective. If it is the case, modify it to be sure it has all the requirements to satisfy your customers' needs. Don't fall into the trap of perfectionism; it will be the feedback from your customers that show you the way to make improvements if they are needed.

Let's suppose you are in front of a doubtful customer, and you have to convince him/her to purchase your product. Besides putting yourself in your customer's shoes, you will also have to learn the art of transformation, which is being able to transform any weaknesses of your product into strengths.

For example, if the customer complains because your price is too high, you will explain that it depends on the particular characteristics of the product that are not present in any other available on the market. Become a skilled transformer, like in the "Transformers" movie of 2007; this will enable you to face any possible objection from your customers.

4 THE IDENTIKIT OF YOUR PRODUCT

Before writing your sales letter, do an Identikit of your product answering the questions of Exercise 4.

EXERCISE 4

1. Make a list in order of priority of at least five benefits that your product offers. What is peculiar about your product? Do not neglect anything. Write everything on a sheet of paper or your PC.

2. Put together all the useful elements that can prove the validity of your offer.

3. Make a list of all your product's benefits, even the secondary ones.

4. How does your product improve the time management of your customer?

5. How does the life of your customer transform after having bought it?

6. What kind of characteristics of your product, your company, and yourself, make your customer want to buy from you?

7. What testimonials from your satisfied customers can you mention to prove that your product solves the problem of your audience?

8. Does any laboratory or another kind of test prove its efficiency?

9. What differentiates your product from the competition? (List at least three differences.)

10. Why would your customer prefer your product instead of one of the competitors?

11. What kind of guarantee are you willing to offer? Within how much time?

12. What are the first words you would say to convince a potential customer to buy your products?

Take your time to answer the question of exercises no. 3 and 4, your answers are fundamental in setting up your winning strategy to be used in your sales letter and the marketing of your company.

5 STEP ONE - THE HEADLINE

Now that you have created the identikit of your ideal customer and your product, you are ready to write the draft of your sales letter. Please go back to Step one of Chapter one of this book. Look at the Headline of the hypothetical Sales Letter of a course entitled "Learn the Art of Winning Sales Letters."

The goal of the headline is to capture the attention of the readers and intrigue them into wanting to find out more. The headline is the first persuasion tool to create curiosity and expectation in the customer's mind. It must be assertive, communicate a specific benefit, such as the resolution of a problem or the achievement of a goal the customer cares for and encourages him or her to discover how to get what he or she wants. Take examples from newspaper headlines and do not be afraid to use appealing words to transmit a significant benefit or make a promise. Without a compelling headline, the reader will lose interest and will not read the rest of your sales letter.

Before you create your headline, write down some examples on a piece of paper or your PC. The answers to the questions in the next exercise will help you to create your captivating headline.

EXERCISE 5

✓ Why should I care about this headline?

✓ Does it make me read the rest of the text?

✓ Does it promise the solution to the problem?

✓ Does it meet my needs?

✓ What emotions does it arouse in me?

✓ Does it encourage me to buy the product?

✓ Is the price adequate compared to the benefits it promises?

Create your style taking inspiration from newspaper headlines or the web, copy some catchy sentences, and change them according to the characteristics of your product. Do all the proof you like and then choose your headline. Even though you are not an expert copywriter, with a little practice, you can write a captivating headline. Train yourself every day until you are satisfied with your style and the way you introduce your product. The more you understand what your customers' goals are, the more chances you have to create an appealing and thrilling text. Give your customers what they need, treat them as if they were one of your best friend or a person you love. Tell them how you managed to solve the problem that afflicts their everyday life, add more testimonials to confirm the effectiveness of your offer.

Enter at least one of the most searched keywords on Google related to the product or service you offer in the headline. Here are some examples of different Headlines.

Example 1. The headline focused on the problem.
FREE YOURSELF FROM, ONCE AND FOR ALL.
"Free yourself from back pain once and for all."
"Free yourself from the usury of the banks forever."
"Free yourself from the urge to smoke using a secret method that has already worked for thousands of people."
"Free yourself from the anxiety of the salary and create from scratch a profitable business."

In this case, your Headline is about a problem and the promise that you make to solve it. The customers will experience every single negative emotion related to it and will be anxious to find out what the solution that you propose is.

Example 2. The headline that asks a question.
WOULD YOU? WHO ELSE WANTS TO?.
"Would you like to live in a beautiful house by the sea and enjoy life?."
"Who else wants to lose weight without dying of hunger?."
"Would you like to enjoy life in your favorite place without the need to work?."
"Who else wants to enjoy the marriage forever, and without stress?."

In contrast to the first example, in this case, the headline anticipates a specific goal, a desire that your customers are eager to achieve, so they will be curious to find out your solution. Your customers are now picturing how their life will improve when they have reached the goal. If you like to use this type of headline, you can start your sales letter describing these positive changes, and then go on talking about the problem in detail, as we will see in the next step.

Example 3. The headline that promises a benefit hard to achieve.

THOUSANDS OF PEOPLE HAVE SUCCESSFULLY, EVEN IF IT SEEMED IMPOSSIBLE

"Thousands of people have been able to overcome the fear of taking a plane, even if it seemed impossible."

"Thousands of people have created a passive income, even if it seemed impossible."

"Thousands of people have overcome panic attacks, even if it seemed impossible."

"Thousands of people passed the pain after their divorce, even when it seemed impossible."

If you choose this headline, you must be sure your product will make the customers achieve a goal that they would not usually achieve because it seemed too complicated for them. In addition to your customers' positive reviews, you need to provide much more evidence to support what you say and demonstrate that other people have achieved the same goal thanks to your method.

Example 4. The headline that increases your customers'

self-esteem.
CREATE A, OF WHICH TO BE PROUD.
"Create a career of which to be proud."
"Create an automatic income to increase your standard of living."
"Open a vegetarian restaurant of which to be proud."
"Reach an emotional balance of which to be proud."

You offer a product that allows the customers to distinguish from other people, achieve excellent results. In this case, your sales letter will propose the most effective strategies to keep the promise you mentioned in the headline.

Example 5. The headline based on urgency.
LEARN HOW TO, IN MINUTES.
"How to lose weight by exercising in half the time."
"How to create a passive income that allows you to retire in 4 years."
"Learn how to become a skilled cook in 24 hours."
"Learn how to make a sale in 10 minutes."

Leveraging on the urgency, you promise a fast and effective solution to improve a particular aspect of your customers' life quickly. Using this type of headline, you demonstrate the effectiveness of your method and the various direct and indirect benefits that the customers will reach in a short time.

In any sales letter, make a list of the positive reviews from your customers who are satisfied with your product. It will increase your reliability and allows you to create an authentic relationship with your future customers.

Other examples of Headlines.

Three unknown strategies to free yourself from __

A little-known secret to ___

How I was able to write a bestseller from a simple idea.

How I increased my self-esteem after reading a motivational book.

How to increase the sales of your company, in seven days.

The five secret properties of pineapple, for weight loss.

The three secret properties of (name of the product), to eliminate fatigue.

Nobody thought I could ever become a CEO, and yet I managed to do it.

Here is the source of eternal youth (product name).

Give me one hour a day, and in a month, you will learn to speak Spanish like Penelope Cruz.

Seven secret strategies to create a successful business from scratch.

To increase the effectiveness of your Headline, you can present it in this way:

- ✓ **Ask a question that introduces the problem (introduction).**
- ✓ **Headline.**
- ✓ **Promise a benefit (sub-headline).**

Examples.

Introduction - Are you tired of having back pain?
Headline - Free yourself from back pain in five simple steps.
Sub-headline - And move your back as easily as when you were a child.
Introduction - Do you want to increase your consulting service sales?
Headline - Discover the three strategies of the winning seller.
Sub-headline - And become one of the highest-paid experts on the market.

Introduction - A solution to the economic crisis?
Headline - Thousands of people had created a passive income even when it seemed impossible.
Sub-headline - And today they are no longer stressed when they have to pay their bills.

Now that you have created your captivating headline, it's time to talk about the problem your customers want to solve.

6 STEP TWO – PRESENTATION OF THE PROBLEM

After the headline, but before describing the problem, some marketing experts introduce themselves to their audience. I prefer to keep the interest alive of those who will read my sales letter for as long as possible, and then to focus immediately on the problem and describe it in a detailed manner. In this phase, you have to "agitate" the problem. Reading your words and the examples you make, the customers will take conscious notes of what happens, and the consequences that they will have to face if they do not take action. Use simple language, speak to the customers as if they were friends that you would like to help at any cost, make them feel understood and accepted, this will help the client to trust you.

Before analyzing the problem, you can ask a question to create a further expectation in the mind of your customers. Questions are an excellent way to form positive mental images and encourage customers to buy your product. Here are some examples to introduce the problem before agitating it.

- ✓ Would you like to enjoy life in a beautiful house by the sea and work only a few hours a day?
- ✓ Would you like to run again, go out with your friends and play with your children, as you did years ago, without suffering from back pain?
- ✓ Imagine being able to communicate effectively with your partner and feel all the pleasant sensations again, just like when you fell in love.

If you decide to break-up the Headline in three parts, as I have suggested before, namely: Introduction – Headline – Sub-headline, there's no need to ask a question immediately after it, or write a sentence that anticipates the final result, because you have already done it by using the sub-headline.

Chapter one of this book, "Learn the Art of Winning Sales Letters," is an example of a sales letter addressed to people who want to increase their sales by learning how to write captivating sales letters. When I began to agitate the problem in the letter, I described the feelings of a person who has not yet achieved the sales volume that he or she would like to. Then, I listed the possible negative situations this person is now experiencing:

- ✓ He is frustrated because he has not reached the sales he expects and deserves.
- ✓ He is tired, worried, and sad because he has not yet reached his goals.

✓ He is so worried because of his future, and that of his family only depends on how many sales he will be able to do.

✓ He has doubts about himself; he thinks that he lacks something essential to increase the sales of his product.

✓ He is depressed because the situation he is currently living in does not change.

I report here a part of the text that I wrote in Chapter one.

"I know how you feel when, after having worked hard, the results you expect are late to arrive. Sometimes your competitors conquer the market, although they have a product that is less valid than yours is. This situation creates frustrations, worry, discomfort, and tiredness.

It is like being trapped inside a hamster wheel; you keep on running without getting anywhere. The uncertainty and doubt prevent you from thinking clearly and finding the right way to increase the sales of your product.

All of this creates stress; maybe you cannot sleep at night. Your future and that of your family depends on the sales you will achieve. You have what it takes to succeed, but you feel something is missing, and despite your commitment, the goal still seems far away."

When the customers have to deal with a problematic situation, agitating the problem helps them to be more aware of what may happen if they do not take any action. Don't be afraid to be harsh in this phase. Clearly describe any possible catastrophic scenario related to the customers' problem. From this moment on, you will start a trusting relationship with your audience, because people will know that you understand the problem too so that they will feel accepted by you. I'm telling you to be harsh because people in trouble tend to be trapped inside a vicious circle, which is difficult to defeat. It's not by chance that fear is the emotion that blocks you the most. It seems strange, but most of the time, human beings make decisions only when they have a great fear of not succeeding anymore. It is always fear, rather than love, that is the element that moves even the most resistant individuals and helps them to change. The momentary discomfort you create when you amplify your customers' concerns will help them to understand that you can make them feel better through the solution you propose.

In case you did not create the product you are selling, you have to become very skillful when you agitate the problem. In any sales letter, but also any other text addressed to your customers, you should always use a simple and understandable language. Pretend you are talking to a child who is around ten years old. Avoid using complicated words, form a logical thread of the subject, always connect one topic to another to avoid unnecessary distractions and confusion. Do simple examples in which your customers can recognize themselves, consider what they think and feel; your words must hypnotize your readers. Use your language to create a scenario in which your reader will identify. Create mental images that are essential to persuade the customers since the human brain mainly works through images.

Other than fear, you can use different strategies of persuasion, such as desire, success, revenge, and recognition, which play a pivotal role in motivation as well.

Here are some examples of phrases you can use to agitate the problem.

- ✓ Have you ever been: frustrated, angry, disappointed, and sad, misunderstood, in a trap, etc.?
- ✓ Have you ever had the feeling of not being able to (describe the goal the customer is not able to reach)?
- ✓ This situation burdens you too much to involve (family, work, colleagues, and friends) describe how these people may suffer the consequences of the problem.
- ✓ Staying faithful to your beliefs will cause you further difficulties because (explain why the ideas of the customer prevent him or her from resolving the problem, e.g., until you do not put yourself in the game, you will never beat your fear of speaking in public, find new customers, follow a proper diet, etc.).
- ✓ Why do you continue to be afraid? (describe what the greatest fear of your customer is and anticipate the solution), e.g., why do you continue to be scared of saying what you think, if now you can attend a course to increase your self-esteem?
- ✓ Any further delay in the resolution of (describe the problem) will cause (make a list of the negative consequences). E.g., further delay in asking for advice from an expert will cause your company to lose thousands of dollars.
- ✓ How would your life be from now on, if you had at your disposal the tools to become an expert in your field? I bet many people will admire you, and other

people will be envious of you because they thought that you would never succeed.

Some examples.
Problem: complicated relationship with your partner.
Agitation: constant argument, stress, frustration, anger, low self-esteem, issues with children, and other members of the family, you no longer want to speak to your partner, because you are convinced that doing so will always end up in a fight.
Solution: your communication course. For example, how to communicate effectively with your partner before going to a lawyer to get a divorce.

Problem: not having enough money to support the family.
Agitation: do not see a way out, fight with the partner, feeling useless; don't believe in your abilities, low self-esteem, resignation, risk of losing your home, or other assets.
Solution: your course to financial freedom. Learn how to create automatic revenues to increase your income each month.

Problem: debilitating back pain.
Agitation: inability to perform even the smallest movements, difficulty staying seated in front of the PC, the impossibility of going out with friends, playing with your children, cleaning the house, standing for more than ten minutes, stress, anxiety, feeling as if you had a disability.
Solution: your postural stretching course to get rid of back pain in a short time.

Now you have learned how to agitate the problem; it is the right time to introduce yourself.

7 STEP THREE – WHY SHOULD THE CUSTOMER TRUST IN YOU

As mentioned in the introduction, people will trust in you first, and then in your product. Other than showing your product in a captivating way, you should introduce yourself, telling your customers how you solved the same problem they are now facing. Acknowledging your experience will increase your credibility and the trust of your audience. Furthermore, the Story Telling technique is one of the most effective methods used by the majority of marketing experts to be well-positioned in the market. It is not by chance that they say that whoever has the best story wins. If you think people are not interested in your own story, you are wrong.

People love to read stories and discover what there is behind your work, knowing how you overcame specific challenges and if there was a particular event that allowed you to reach a goal, even when you thought you couldn't succeed. All of these elements add value to your offering and make you look like the most qualified person to solve the problem. In this case, your self-esteem will help you to be fearless and expose the facts in a certain way.

You don't have to brag but talk about your experience to motivate your customers to improve and convince them that, like you, they can reach a specific goal too. The question I would like you to answer now is: **"How can I prove people will get excellent results thanks to my product?."** Your customers are curious individuals, and they will become even more curious knowing what you have done to overcome the same difficulties they are now taking on. So if you can do something useful, why not tell your audience?

In order not to miss anything important when you write your personal story, answer the questions in the next exercise.

EXERCISE 6

1. What difficulties did you face because of the problem?
2. What emotions, feelings, and thoughts did you have when you needed to solve it?
3. Were you forced to do something that you didn't want to do?
4. How were, at that moment, your relationships with the people you loved, with your work colleagues, your employees, your work partners?
5. What drove you to resolve the problem? Describe a particular event, emotion, or something that you were able to understand that allowed you to find the solution.
6. What did you do exactly when you decided to solve the problem?

7. Did you ask for help from someone else, or did you read books or attend courses that helped you?
8. What were the ideals, the passions, or the desires that encouraged you to act?
9. Are they the same ideals that allowed you to create the product you offer now?
10. What benefits did you get by using the product you are offering now?
11. Why should your product be useful to others?
12. Why should people trust you and buy from you?
13. What are the emotions that your product arouses in people?

After reading your personal story, your audience will perceive both yourself and your product in a different way; they will know how hard you worked to create an effective solution for them, and the various difficulties you had to face to succeed. Your customers begin to know and trust you, so I suggest you always tell real facts. Even those who don't know you and read your content for the first time can guess if you are telling the truth or not.

Every time you think appropriate, clearly write in your sales letter that the results your customers will obtain exclusively depend on how much they will be willing to commit to getting what they want. The following examples guide you through creating your story; write using a simple and captivating style.

In your customer's shoes. In the past, you lived a similar experience to that of your customer, so you describe the moments you were in the same situation, the emotions you felt, what obstacles you had to overcome, and if there was an event or an insight that allowed you to find the solution to the problem. For example, you suffered from back pain for a long time, you almost could not move, and no physician had ever given you useful advice. Later, you decided to follow a course of postural stretching, and your back pain disappeared. You then created a video training course of postural stretching to get rid of back pain.

From rags to riches. You lived in a worse situation than your customer lives now. For example, you were left with no money because your company went bankrupt, consequently to the economic crisis. Then, your partner and your friends abandoned you. Describe how you got away from that terrible situation, how you managed to open a new financial consultancy, which today guarantees you excellent incomes.

For this reason, you may offer your customer a subscription to a financial advisory service. On the other hand, you risked your life because of a severe illness, and then you wrote a book in which you tell how you healed yourself. Any traumatic experience you have lived through, after reaching the bottom of the barrel, you explain how you rose again.

Reveal the hidden secret. You worked in a particular industry for a long time, and you learned the tricks of the trade. Then, you tell your readers what mistakes to avoid in a specific sector. For example, you worked in a bank, so now you can create a video course to explain how not to be fooled by the banking system, e.g., how to save most of the

50% of bank charges by paying attention to particular items on the bank account bill.

The top expert. You worked in a specific industry for a long time, and you experienced all sorts of things. You know every trick, error, strategy, even those of your competitors, and you have become one of the most respected experts in your field. That's why you are the right person to satisfy the requirements of your customers.

The passionate researcher. You spent so much time studying a particular topic; you attended courses, read books, and spoken with the leading experts. Your researches have enabled you to create an innovative product to improve your customers' lives. For example, you can offer a cookery course, a course on how to learn to speak in public or learn how to play a musical instrument.

In Chapter One, I told you how I felt when I was doing a job I didn't love. I found my way only when I decided to follow my passions. If I had not done it, I would have never understood that the marketing and the persuasion strategies are crucial for success, and to be loved by your audience. In Chapter one, I used this sentence, "*Who would have ever thought that Elena Adani, who when she was a teenager had bad self-esteem and was often teased by others because she was too introverted, would have been able to take back the power of her own life and make such a radical change?*" With this sentence, I wanted my audience to understand that every person, even those who do not have high self-confidence, can change their lives when they decide to do so. And they can learn how to write captivating sales letters, to communicate effectively, achieve success, and be admired by their audience.

If you have not created the product you sell, I recommend you test it on yourself first, to understand its potential, and describe it accurately in your sales letter. In this case, instead of telling your personal story, you can mention the positive review of one of your satisfied customers, asking to describe in detail all the benefits that he or she noticed after using it.

8 STEP FOUR – INTRODUCE YOUR SOLUTION

Now it's time to let your customers discover all the details of your offer. From this moment on, you will mainly base your sales letters on persuasion.

You may have even told a touching personal story to your audience. However, your customers may still have doubts and won't be convinced to buy from you. I want to give you an example of a problematic customer because one day, you will have to deal with stubborn or distrustful individuals. For this reason, I recommend that you re-read the answers you gave in exercise three as they are useful to remind you which thoughts and limiting beliefs block your customers from reaching a specific goal.

Before going on to prove that your product works and it is the most suitable one for your customers, do this experiment. Pretend you do not know anything about your product and answer these questions.

✓ What emotions, thoughts, and images do this product arouse in me?
✓ What would I think if I was seeing the product for the first time?

You may have difficulties to distance yourself from it. In

this case, ask at least three people to respond to these questions and honestly tell you what they think of your product. This additional test is helpful as a further check-up before you introduce your product to the market; this will give you a precise idea about how it will be perceived.

You can use all the marketing strategies that you know, write the most eye-catching sales letter you can, but other than persuasion, you must be skillful at understanding how the market on which you'll be focusing will perceive your product.

If your product is similar to one on the market in your industry, don't copy the marketing strategy and don't strive to become a leader too, because it's worthless. On the contrary, it will be more useful you identify the characteristics of your product that differentiate it from the competition and base your sales strategy on these elements. Being the first to win in a particular niche will bring you advantages over trying to become a global leader from scratch.

Now your customers are waiting to know the advantages of the solution you are suggesting. Highlight the aspects that make it different from others. You, your story, and your product, you must be DIFFERENT and not the BEST because the concept of best is relative.

Here's an example.

If I ask you, what are the top five toothpaste brands that come into your mind? Indeed, you would not respond "Lavera." Lavera is a German company that since 1987 produces completely natural cosmetics and personal hygiene products without any chemical additive. However, if I now ask the same question to individuals who are fans of wellness, and regularly visit supermarkets that sell organic products, Lavera would probably be one of the first brands of toothpaste that people would remember.

Have you noticed what the difference is? Lavera primarily addresses to an attentive audience that respects the environment and uses products that do not contain any chemical additive harmful to the body. As you can see, the mass does not perceive Lavera as one of the best toothpaste manufacturers; instead, an audience with a specific interest considers it one of the leading companies of high-quality natural products, toothpaste included.

So, what are the unique characteristics of your product that cannot be found in others on which you can create a winning text to convince your customers to buy from you?

Your uniqueness is your strength, so while you are writing your sales letter, highlight it as much as you can.

For example, you may have discovered the winning formula to earn money online in a particular industry by investing little money, or you may have invented a long-lasting natural product to dye your hair. You may be an accountant expert in a tax-saving system for farms, etc.

In a world full of offers of any kind and companies that are struggling to survive, sometimes you just need a different element to enter into the heart of a specific group of people.

Besides, there is nothing wrong if you admit you are not the leader. Instead, concentrate on creating a captivating pay-off, which is one slogan containing the promise the competition does not offer.

Examples.

We are the no. 2 in fast food, so why choose us? Because we sell hamburgers made of organic meat.

I'm not the most famous marketing consultant in the world, but none of the ones that you will find on the market will teach you how to be successful in sales by increasing your self-esteem.

There are many biscuits brands available in supermarkets, so why choose our brand? Because unlike others, our cookies are the only ones that do not contain any sugar, salt, nor palm oil.

Another seemingly counterintuitive technique to express your uniqueness is the **strategy of imperfection**. Many marketing experts use this trick when they describe their product; they admit any flaw or defect of it. The truth is the sale always depends on the customers' needs, and therefore, any possible imperfection of your product can become an advantage.

For example, some people might not be attracted by the idea of going out and eating in an essential restaurant, attended by ordinary people, where there are no waiters dressed with livery and in which you can only choose a few dishes. On the other hand, this option might be interesting for other people. In any case, the strategy of imperfection can create disinterest for some people, while for others, it will be exciting. That's the reason why it is an excellent strategy to select your audience from now on and gives you the possibility to anticipate and respond to any objections. Furthermore, this technique allows you to demonstrate your sincerity, thus consolidating the relationship of trust that you're creating with your readers.

Here are some examples.

If you want to take a vacation in an expensive tourist village, spending all day within the structure, obliged to comply with a precise schedule, getting involved from the animators, even when you don't want to, without the possibility of interaction with the culture of the place, then our Bed and Breakfast is not for you. However, if you like to stay in a typical Bed and Breakfast surrounded by nature, completely renovated, a few meters from the sea, and visit independently the beautiful beaches and the monasteries of the island of Samos, eat where you want without the worry of time, without spending a fortune, then our Bed and Breakfast is for you.

You can contact a famous lawyer in a beautiful office and wait a long time before having an appointment and getting the information you need, only then to be forced to take a loan from the bank to pay the fee, without any guarantee of success. However, if you want an immediate appointment with a lawyer, even in an ordinary office, who quickly responds to your request at any time, without having to spend a fortune, then our legal department is for you.

Let yourself be tempted by the brand of supplements you prefer that promise you to lose 10 kg. in a month without effort, eating all that you want. Live this dream, but then do not complain if you do not get the result you expected. If you like to permanently lose weight and understand the causes of your metabolism slowing down, our expert nutritionists will create a customized dietary program for you, including 100% natural supplements from our company to lose weight without stress.

Use the style you prefer when you introduce your product, and become skilled in transforming any imperfection into strengths, on which basing your marketing strategy.

9 STEP FIVE – INTRODUCE YOUR PRODUCT

Most of the time, it is not the best product that wins on the market but the marketing strategy used by the leading company. Sometimes leaders sell average or low-quality products. McDonald's, for example, has become the leader of fast food while not selling high-quality hamburgers (in my opinion). The fact is the objective reality does not exist because each person interprets it differently. Like the real world, even the world of marketing is made of perceptions and decisions based on different points of view. The majority of people are convinced of having an excellent ability to make choices and good deals.

Furthermore, you have to consider the trends of the moment. Often people buy because they trust in the opinion of others or because they do not like to feel inferior to those who possess a particular type of object. In any case, there is not a suitable product for everyone, and that's why I suggest you not to waste too much time making it perfect if you are ready to sell it. The feedback from your customers will provide you with the elements you need to carry out changes if necessary.

Now it's time to introduce your product.

Choose the name or the title carefully, the more captivating, the better and remember the promise you made in the Headline, this will give you more chance of success.

Please re-read the answer you gave to exercise no. 4 about your product's Identikit, then describe it following the steps of the next exercise.

EXERCISE 7

1. Describe your product and explain how it will improve the life of your customers by listing at least five benefits.
2. Describe any secondary benefits, how will the product improve other aspects of the customers' life that are not directly related to the main advantages? For example: in addition to losing weight, our supplements will increase your energy so you will feel less tired.
3. Explain its exclusive features, the ones that the customers will never find in other similar products of the competition — for example, biscuits without sugar, salt, and palm oil.
4. Always add some elements that allow you to demonstrate an economic advantage, for example, save time, money, avoid difficulties that could be very hard to overcome, etc.

If you have other ideas, add examples to prove the validity of your product, you can take inspiration from the following sentences.

✓ Create (name of the goal) from zero through various stages.
✓ Motivate… to do ... to get.
✓ You will get.. That will give you ... so you can.
✓ Present an eye-catching … to convince.

✓ Transform the limitations into strengths.

✓ Save you thousands of dollars because you can... Thanks ...

✓ Avoid making these mistakes... you would not lose (time, money, opportunities, etc).

✓ Learn the tricks of .... to reach ...

Even though you are offering an ordinary product, show it off as if it were unique. If you are providing a service or a course of any type, clearly specify that the constant commitment of the customer is required to reach the result. If instead, you sell a particular or technologic object, you will recommend your customers read the instructions carefully, and in your sales letter, you'll specify in which cases it is preferable not to use it as it may cause side effects.

To avoid any misunderstandings with your readers, after the product's description, I suggest you make a clear distinction between the type of people that are more suitable to use your product and those less suitable, creating two kinds of bullet lists. The first list will be titled "This product (name) is for people who," while the second list will have a title like "This product (name) is not for people who."

Let's take the example of a marketing course for learning how to write winning sales letters. After having described the benefits that the customers will get by attending it, you write to whom the course is for or is not for.

Warning, the course "Learn the Art of Winning Sales Letters" is for people who:

✓ Are willing to learn the most effective sales techniques.
✓ Want to increase their sales.
✓ Want to improve communication with customers.
✓ Want to have the necessary tools to consult with their marketing teams.
✓ Want to become a marketing consultant.

However, this course is not for people who:
✓ Are not willing to undertake the marketing of their company.
✓ Do not want to learn the rules of persuasion.
✓ Are convinced that just having a good product is enough to sell it.
✓ Ignore the importance of sales letters and winning communication in their marketing strategy.
✓ Completely delegate their marketing strategies to marketing agencies or consultants without giving their support.
✓ Are convinced that their personal story and experiences are not interesting for their audience.
✓ Feel worthless to create a trust relationship with their potential customers.

Now you might think that by making this distinction you will lose a part of your potential customers.

While reading this part of your sales letter, some people could realize they are no more interested in your product, so they may decide to let go when they read the list "This product is not for."

In my opinion, it's more convenient to acquire customers

willing to commit rather than interact with people who do not, so these bullet lists will allow you to already make the first selection of your customers in this phase.

When I made the first list in the previous example, I concentrated on the concept of "responsibility," saying that if an entrepreneur wants to be successful, he or she should never neglect the marketing of his or her company. If you had been a part of the second list, you would not be here to read these words. I congratulate you because if you have reached this point, it means that you carefully thought about the importance of marketing and communication.

After having presented your product, it is time to communicate its price.

10 STEP SIX – PRICE AND BONUSES

During this step of your sales letter, your self-esteem will be helpful more than ever, mainly when you communicate the price with no hesitation. You worked so hard to create your product or to sell one of the others, so it's right that the customers pay a fair price. If you are going to offer a favorable price, and if the customers are convinced that he or she will get a higher value than the amount he or she will pay, you have more chances to conclude the sale.

There is nothing wrong saying that your offer is very convenient, in comparing your price to other more expensive similar products. When you introduce the price, take inspiration from the following sentences.

✓ You'll see that the cost of all of this will be less than you expect.

✓ This is a special offer at an incredibly low price.

✓ Take advantage of this offer and get your (product name) for the incredible price of...

✓ Don't miss the opportunity to close the more advantageous deal of your life at the special price of...

✓ Why throwing away thousands of dollars on expensive products/services/consultancy when you can have everything you want at a very competitive price?

✓ Why doing everything by yourself and waste your time and your money unnecessarily, if now you have everything you need to save time/money/hours of study?

✓ Hurry up and take advantage of this offer because it will only be valid until (date), and now get the (name the product) at the exclusive price of...

Your offer will not end with the price, but it will continue. You are writing an eye-catching sales letter to sell your product; you have to use all possible strategies to get your reader to complete the purchase. One of these strategies requires you include in your offer some free bonuses.

The objective of the bonus is not to encourage the customers to say "Yes" but to make your customers pronounce these words: "I can't wait anymore, and I want it now!"

Offer bonuses that increase the utility, reliability, and applicability of your product and, when possible, also the speed in achieving a specific goal. The gifts amplify the value of your offer, and the customers will be convinced that you are proposing a good deal.

There are various types of bonuses depending on the type of product, for example, you can give for free:

✓ A part of the product, for example, the first chapter of a book, the first part of a video course.
✓ A free consultation.
✓ An accessory that completes the product.
✓ A free of charge service for a specified period.
✓ The possibility to attend for free the same course for the second time.
✓ Free membership for a specified period.
✓ Another product as a gift.

It is crucial always to specify the economic value of each

bonus that you offer. After the price, make a list of the gifts, describe them in detail, and use the bullet points if needed. Then add the product price to the cost of the bonuses. Now you have a higher amount than that of your offer, so from this total deduct the value of the bonuses, then you get the final price of your product.

Example.
Why throw away thousands of dollars paying high prices for legal advice, when you can have it at an affordable price? Take advantage of the offer of our legal office and book your consulting at the special price of

$ 150,00

But that's not all; the price includes:
Bonus no.1 a free guide written in a simple way that will explain to you how to avoid financial scams,

value $ 100,00+

Bonus no.2 a second consulting free of charge

value $ 150,00=

Total Bonuses Price $ 250,00

TOTAL $ 400,00

Of course, you will not have to pay $ 400,00.

You will get the two consultancies plus the guide to avoid financial scams at the incredible price of

$ 150,00

Now you have revealed your incredibly reasonable price. Let's suppose once again that your customers still have doubts and are not willing to buy. So, after releasing the price, you will not allow them to rest even for a second and abandon reading your sales letter. Your customers must not have a moment to think about whether to accept or refuse your proposal. If you give your customers this time, you will lose them forever. Avoid such a situation, using the most powerful strategies of sale, **urgency, and scarcity**.

Every effective sales letter always shows the expiration date of the offer (urgency) or that a particular product is available until a specific time, after which you can no longer purchase it (scarcity). Depending on the type of product you sell, tell your customers the expiration date of your offer or the limited availability of your product. You can use the following sentences to do so.

- ✓ Don't let this fantastic offer getaway. After the (date), the price will increase, and I still have not decided if, in the future, there will be another discount on (name of the product).
- ✓ After the (date), the stocks will be finished, and the bonus of this offer will be not available anymore.
- ✓ You can't find this unique offer anywhere else at this price so that it will be available only until (date).
- ✓ This method is the result of my long experience in the sector (name of industry), and you'll never find any other product similar to what I'm offering now at such a low price.
- ✓ How many people today know the (name of the product) and can resolve (describe the problem)? Take

action now if you want to be part of a wealthy elite that will know the secret strategies that no one else has ever revealed before today.

Now that you have specified the conditions of your offer, the distrust of your customers will start to decrease. To convince them to trust you and your product, even more, share some positive reviews from your satisfied customers.

11 STEP SEVEN – REVIEWS

Reviews are critical to proving that your product works and that you have told the truth. People trust other people's opinions, and your satisfied customers will confirm that.

If you have not yet received positive reviews of your product, get in touch with some of your most loyal customers and ask them to write a review. Make sure that they tell you how they solved their problem by using your product and ask them to describe any other positive results that they have achieved thanks to it. The reviews should be complete with the picture of your customers, so you need to obtain their permission to publish them. If you have some video reviews, include them in your sales letter. Videos are more effective compared to written text. If you have difficulties in getting the reviews, use free bonuses, such as an ebook or a consultancy, to convince your customers to write them.

Avoid publishing false opinions or from your friends and acquaintances that have not yet tried your product. As you have noticed, in Chapter one, I did not write any review of the course "Learn the Art of Winning Sales Letters." I could have added some reviews, but I did not because I prefer to tell the truth, saying that the course is new on the market (September 2019) so it is impossible it has already received some comments by the customers.

If it is the first time you have launched your product on the market, and you still haven't received positive feedbacks, you can say it. I always prefer to tell the truth, so it is up to you how to manage reviews.

If you think appropriate, offer an additional free bonus to those who will be willing to write a review after having tried your product. Truth is always the best option. Of course, without reviews, at the beginning of your marketing campaign, you may have less visibility. However, it is better waiting for the right time to be known in the market, rather than appearing suddenly full of non-trusting positive reviews. In any case, you can always offer a guarantee to refund customers if they are not fully satisfied with your product.

12 STEP EIGHT – GUARANTEE

You put all your efforts into creating a unique product, and you answered all the possible objections of your readers, and you came up to this point in your sales letter, and you are sure you've done an excellent job. Surely you have given the best of you. However, every person thinks differently to others, so despite the validity of your product, some customers might not be fully satisfied with it, and may ask for a refund.

To give further trust to the purchasers and safeguard the reputation of the seller, the majority of sales letters include a guarantee. As your customers know that they are buying a product covered by a warranty, they will feel safe and know that they do not risk anything, so they will be more willing to buy. Sometimes, entrepreneurs offer a guarantee of a higher value than the same product because they are so sure about the effectiveness of it that they do not expect any refund request.

In most cases, the guarantee consists of giving the customers their money back, and when expected, the return of the product with no charges for the customers.

As a guarantee, some companies offer another product or service of a higher value than the price the customer has paid, i.e., consulting, a pre-paid shopping cart, or other.

In any case, the return of the money is the most used procedure that will protect your customers more than others. Usually, the guarantee includes a 30-days limit; within this, the customer is allowed to ask for it.

The following examples are about phrases you can use to describe the guarantee.

✓ If you purchase our financial management course, we guarantee a 30% saving on taxes, if you do not get these results within 60 days, we will refund you the price you paid.

✓ In our restaurant, you will be served in 10 minutes. Otherwise, we will refund the price of your dish.

✓ After attending our course (name of the course) last year more than 1000 salesmen have increased their sales. If you do not increase your sales even by a dollar, we will refund the entire price within 30 days.

✓ I am so confident that my product (name of the product) will work beyond your expectations, that I'm tempted not to apply any guarantee. However, if you are not satisfied with it, I will refund you the entire price within 30 days.

✓ If, after this course (name of the course) you do not achieve any improvement in the communication with your customers, you will get 100% of your money back within 30 days.

In case you have already obtained many positive reviews, and you are sure of the potential of your product, you can offer a guarantee that promises the customers to reach a specific goal within a particular time.

13 STEP NINE – SUMMARY

Up to this point, your sales letter should be long enough, so it is useful to make a general summary, highlighting the most critical parts of your proposal. Do not be afraid to repeat the same concepts often; your readers are not always careful; sometimes, they are in a hurry, so they may not remember everything that you have said until now.

EXERCISE 8

1. Describe the problem of your customers again, and agitate it.
2. Introduce your solution, describing the benefits that your customers will get by buying your product.
3. Explain what the features of your product are and those that differentiate it from the competition.
4. Repeat the total price that includes free bonuses.
5. Compare your price with other similar products, specifying how much money, time, work, study, etc., will save your customers through your product.
6. Point out the urgency and exclusivity of your offer, also set the expiry date.
7. Remind your readers to look at the testimonials of your satisfied customers.
8. Confirm the conditions of your guarantee.

Examples.
   Why not learn to communicate effectively with your partner avoiding arguments once and for all. Are you

treating each other as you were enemies, feeling anger, sadness, and frustration?

To avoid making an appointment with your lawyer to file for divorce, the communication course (name of the course) is what you are looking for. In this course, I will reveal the most effective NPL and coaching techniques and how to manage disagreement. Indeed you can learn all of these techniques in other classes, perhaps taught by gurus more famous than me, but none of them will give you practical self-esteem lessons. Having good lasting relationships with all the people you love without an ounce of self-esteem, it is impossible.

So, why are you wasting your time in courses that do not teach self-esteem?

The course ... today is available at a special price ...

But it is not all; the cost is approximately 30% lower than other similar courses on the market. It also includes:

BONUS 1   Live chat with our expert for all the course time, value $...

BONUS 2 Possibility to attend for free this course at the time you want, value $...

If, after having attended the course and practicing our techniques every day, you do not achieve any improvement in the relationship with your partner, don't worry, I will refund you the entire price.

Hurry up!!! The course ... will be available at a special price of ... for just a few days from the (date of expiry), then the price will increase, and I still have not decided when and if there will be other special offers like this once again. Why don't you follow your heart and take advantage of this incredible offer?

Your salary is not enough, every day you are struggling to pay the bills and all the expenses of your family, and you want to give them a decent future because they deserve it. We are not asking you for a thousand dollars investment, you only need 200 $ to start using our platform, and in a few months, your investment will triple. There are hundreds of other investments available now, but none of these will guarantee you a three weeks training to learn the secrets of the "BitCoin."

Invest only 200$ on our platform (name), and if you do not get at least 600$ in a couple of months, you will be refunded. No other company will allow you to earn money using such a small initial investment.

Why don't you invest your first 200$ to your financial freedom? This offer includes an initial three weeks training to discover all the secrets on how to triple your investment, but that's not all, it will also include:

BONUS 1 an online guide to learn all the secrets of the BitCoin, worth $
BONUS 2 a free consultation with one of our experts, worth $

Are you waiting for your salary increase by itself? Do not miss this opportunity because from (date), the minimum required amount for this investment will change, and we do not know when and if there will be other offers in the future. Follow your heart, and call this number ...now.

Does getting rid of weight seem impossible to you?

Have you already spent a fortune on diets, supplements that at the beginning helped you to lose kilos, but then in a short time you went back to your initial weight?

Before losing hope, read what I'm about to tell you carefully. The problem is not the diets or the supplements you will find on the market, and it's not even your will, because I'm sure you've put your heart and soul into following a diet. The problem is that no one will explain the cause of your metabolism slowing down, and this what prevents you from losing weight.

In our program (name of the program), an expert nutritionist will take care of you every day with a customized diet, which is based on specific blood tests.

From today onwards, you will not be forced to throw your money from the window anymore in useless diets and supplements to take without following any logic.

Take advantage of this offer today and get the weight loss program (name) at the special price of $ ...

But that's not all; the price also includes:

BONUS 1   Three Coaching sessions with our expert to support you during your weight loss journey value $

BONUS 2   Two supplement packs coadjuvant of the program ... value $

Before it's too late, take advantage of this exclusive offer now. You have a short time to do it because tomorrow the price will go up and we do not know when Dr. ..., the CEO of our Company, will start a new promotion with other discounts.

14 STEP TEN – CALL TO ACTION

You have finally arrived at the final part of your sales letter. You now have your last chance to push your customers to buy. As we have seen before, emotions play a fundamental role in the sale; the majority of people think of being highly skilled in choosing good deals. In this step of your sales letter use emotional logic to eliminate any possible barrier in your customers' minds, allow them to take the decisive action to conclude the sale. Remind your customers that:

✓ The guarantee will protect them, so they do not risk anything.

✓ Some reviews confirm the validity of your product.

✓ Your product is entirely different from all of the others. Repeat why only your product is the most suitable to your customers, and how your customers' lives will improve after having tried it. For example, your customers will save time/money/ or avoid specific inconveniences.

✓ They will be able to reach the goal that they want quickly, without wasting time.

✓ The positive emotions they will feel as soon as they have tried your product.

Create an incisive **Call to Action** to encourage your customers to accept your offer, get inspired by the following sentences.

✓ Trust yourself and make the first step to your freedom from (e.g., back pain, overweight, financial problems, etc.) and take action now by clicking here.

✓ Believe what other people say of (name of the product) and take advantage of this incredible offer.

✓ You know that you will regret it if you do not take the opportunity to buy (name of the product) at the special price of $...

✓ If you carefully look inside yourself, you know that you want (name of the product), so what are you waiting for? Transform your life now.

✓ You've already lost too much precious time, buy it now by clicking here.

Tell your customers not to waste more time because your offer is time-limited, so repeat once again its expiring date or tell that the product is available in limited quantities. That's the reason why your customers should not miss the opportunity to get it immediately.

If you have created a sales letter on the web after the call to action, insert a button (usually red or blue) to allow the readers to make the purchase. When they click that button, they will be directed to a page where they can pay for the product by using the Credit card, Pay Pal, or a bank transfer. If your product is expensive, give the opportunity of paying it by installments.

15 STEP ELEVEN – CONCLUSION

You can finish your sales letter by adding a P.S.

It can be a summary the customers will get from your offer or a list of disadvantages they will have if they do not own your product. Then, analyze the part of your sales letter in which you "agitated" the problem and described the benefits of your offer.

Decide on which emotions to base your conclusion on if you recall the negative ones related to the problem or the positive emotions related to the benefits the customers will get after the purchase. Even though you are repeating concepts that you have already highlighted before, using the P.S. you have the opportunity to provide a summary of the essential points of your message.

After the P.S. end your sales letter by thanking your customers for having read it, give the impression that you already know them. Wish them luck in achieving his or her goals, even in case they will not purchase your product. Confirm that you always will be at their disposal for any information they may ask. Write your email address, the name of your site, and if you like, give your customers a contact phone number so that you can be reached.

Invite your customers to visit your website, and look at other products or services you offer, and insert a link to these products. Send your greetings and sign your letter.

16 RECAP

As we have seen in Chapter two of this book, "Learn the Art of Winning Sales Letters," the importance of self-esteem in the sales process is crucial. When the seller reaches good self-esteem, high-quality energy manifests, even at a subconscious level. This energy can help the seller to have more chances to close the sale and be able to enter into the mind of the customers, to understand their deepest desires.

If you want to increase your sales, I recommend you use all the tools that are available to reach good self-esteem. Then choose in which market niche you would like to work with, and what kind of audience you would like to address. Concentrate on your customers to create an identikit of them, understand what their needs are and how your product can satisfy them.

After choosing a captivating title for your product or service, and having made a list of its essential characteristics, specifically the ones that differentiate it from the competitors, then you are ready to write your winning sales letter.

In step one of this course, we considered the importance of creating a captivating headline, able to stimulate the curiosity in the reader. Then, we took into consideration headline styles and how to divide it into three parts (Introduction – Headline and Sub-headline). After the headline, you talk about the problem and agitate it as I have shown in step two, so the customers will come face to face with their greatest fears, and understand what they risk if they do not take any action to solve the problem.

As I said in the introduction, people will trust you first, and then your product. More than introducing your offer attractively, in step three, you have to introduce yourself to your customers by telling them how you solved the same problem that they are facing. Add any important detail to make the readers understand all the difficulties you had to overcome and what ideas you had when you created the product that you offer. Providing your personal experiences will be useful to raise your reliability and increase trust from your audience.

In steps four and five, we saw how to introduce your product and explain its unique features and what makes it different from the competitors. If there are already leading companies in your industry, do not fall into the competition and want to become the leader of your specific field, on the contrary, concentrate on the particularity and uniqueness of your product, and build on these elements your marketing strategy.

Step six was dedicated to the price and the free bonuses, these are vitally important for the customers to consider your offer seriously and prefer it to others. Use urgency or scarcity by setting an expiring time of your proposal. You can also use the low availability of your product, to create a sense of urgency, this will push the customers to buy it immediately, without allowing them to think of it for a long time.

The reviews from satisfied customers you will insert in step seven after the price will help you to consolidate the trust relationship that you are creating with your readers. If you do not have positive reviews yet, because the product on sale is new to the market, you can add additional bonuses for those who will be willing to give you a positive review, which should always be complete with a photo, or even better a video.

As I showed in step eight, to make your customers feel safe and prove your reliability, always provide a guarantee, which is essentially the total refund of the product's price.

In step nine, we made a general summary of what we had written up to that moment, speaking briefly about the problem, the benefits of your product, price, and exclusive bonuses of the offer.

Step ten was dedicated to the Call to action, such as to invite the customers to purchase. You tell them that they wouldn't want to miss the opportunity that you have offered, and you encourage them to immediately proceed with the purchase, confirming that your solution is the most suitable to achieve a specific goal. If you create a sales letter online, add a button that the customers can click to jump into a page in which they will complete the purchase by choosing the payment method that they prefer.

In step eleven about the conclusion, you can end your sales letter by adding a P.S. listing the problems or the benefits the customers will obtain to help with the decision to purchase the product. Thank the customers and put yourself at their complete disposal by providing your email address, your website, and if you want a phone number.

Now it is up to you to create a unique product or service, able to solve a specific problem, or how to differentiate your existing product from the others already available on the market.

As I have told you several times during this book, it's your uniqueness, the added value, and your availability to listen to your customers and satisfy even the most pretentious ones that make the difference.

To conquer your place in the market, creating something innovative is not enough; you always have to risk your reputation in front of your customers. Therefore, if you are not convinced of what you sell, if you have doubts and do not feel to commit fully, I recommend you to stop, reflect and then decide what the best road to follow is. Sometimes it is easy to lose faith and enthusiasm, especially when you have to strive for success, and that's the reason why I told you about self-esteem at the beginning.

I invite you to contact Kevin and me on the website https://lifenowacademy.com to take advantage of the free test you can download from the site or request an online business coaching free consultation.

Kevin and I have decided to offer this free consultation to the readers of this book. What are you waiting for?

Contact us using this email address: elena@lifenowacademy.com and get your free consultation.

www.ingramcontent.com/pod-product-compliance
Lightning Source LLC
Chambersburg PA
CBHW071028220526
45467CB00004B/1564